Preventing Skin Problems from Working with Portland Cement

U.S. Department of Labor

Occupational Safety and Health Administration

OSHA 3351-07
2008

I0473205

Contents

Portland cement is a generic term used to describe a variety of building materials valued for their strong adhesive properties when mixed with water. Employees who work with portland cement are at risk of developing skin problems, ranging from mild and brief to severe and chronic.

Wet portland cement can damage the skin because it is caustic, abrasive, and absorbs moisture. Portland cement also contains trace amounts of hexavalent chromium [Cr(VI)], a toxin harmful to the skin. Dry portland cement is less hazardous to the skin because it is not as caustic as wet cement.

The purpose of this document is to make employers and employees aware of the skin problems associated with exposure to portland cement; to note the OSHA standards that apply to work with portland cement; and to provide guidance on how to prevent cement-related skin problems. Measures to protect employees from inhalation and eye hazards associated with exposure to portland cement are also noted.

Who is at Risk

Any employee who has skin contact with wet portland cement has the potential to develop cement-related skin problems. Portland cement is an ingredient in the following materials:

- concrete
- mortar
- plaster
- grout
- stucco
- terrazzo

There are many different tasks that involve the use of portland cement. Examples of employees who may be exposed to the dangers of wet portland cement products include bricklayers, carpenters, cement masons, concrete finishers, hod carriers,[1] laborers, plasterers, tile setters, terrazzo workers, ready-mixed concrete truck drivers, bucket and buggy operators, and those involved in pouring and finishing work.

Skin Problems Caused by Exposure to Portland Cement

Wet portland cement can cause caustic burns, sometimes referred to as cement burns. Cement burns may result in blisters, dead or hardened skin, or black or green skin. In severe cases, these burns may extend to the bone and cause disfiguring scars or disability.

Employees cannot rely on pain or discomfort to alert them to cement burns because cement burns may not cause immediate pain or discomfort. By the time an employee becomes aware of a cement burn, much damage has already been done. Cement burns can get worse even after skin contact with cement has ended. Any employee experiencing a cement burn is advised to see a health care professional immediately.

Skin contact with wet portland cement can also cause inflammation of the skin, referred to as dermatitis. Signs and symptoms of dermatitis can include itching, redness, swelling, blisters, scaling, and other changes in the normal condition of the skin.

Contact with wet portland cement can cause a non-allergic form of dermatitis (called irritant contact dermatitis) which is related to the caustic, abrasive, and drying properties of portland cement.

In addition, Cr(VI) can cause an allergic form of dermatitis (allergic contact dermatitis, or ACD) in sensitized employees who work with wet portland cement. When an employee is sensitized, that person's immune system overreacts to small amounts of Cr(VI), which can lead to severe inflammatory reactions upon subsequent exposures. Sensitization may result from a single Cr(VI) exposure, from repeated exposures over the course of months or years, or it may not occur at all. After an employee becomes sensitized, brief skin contact with very small amounts of Cr(VI) can trigger ACD.

ACD is long-lasting and employees can remain sensitized to Cr(VI) years after their exposure to portland cement has ended. Medical tests (e.g., skin patch tests) are available that can confirm whether an employee has become dermally sensitized to Cr(VI).

Employees who work with wet portland cement and experience skin problems, including seemingly minor ones, are advised to see a health care professional for evaluation and treatment. In cement-related dermatitis, early diagnosis and treatment can help prevent chronic skin problems.

SEE A HEALTH CARE PROFESSIONAL IF YOU WORK WITH WET PORTLAND CEMENT AND HAVE SKIN PROBLEMS!!

OSHA Standards Applicable to Working with Portland Cement

Several OSHA standards require employers to take steps to protect employees from hazards associated with exposure to portland cement. These standards include requirements for:

Personal Protective Equipment (29 CFR 1926 Subpart E for construction; 29 CFR 1910 Subpart I for general industry; 29 CFR 1915 Subpart I for shipyards)

OSHA's personal protective equipment (PPE) standards require that PPE be provided, used, and maintained in a sanitary and reliable condition whenever it is necessary to protect employees from injury or impairment. The employer must provide PPE such as boots and gloves as necessary and appropriate for jobs involving exposure to portland cement and ensure these items are maintained in a sanitary and reliable condition when not in use. Employees must be able to clean or exchange PPE if it becomes ineffective or contaminated on the inside with portland cement while in use. In addition, employers are required to provide PPE at no cost to their employees with limited exceptions (1910.132(h)).

Sanitation (29 CFR 1926.51 for construction; 29 CFR 1910.141 for general industry; 29 CFR 1915.97 for shipyards)

Construction employers must make washing facilities available for employees exposed to portland cement. Washing facilities must provide clean water, non-alkaline soap, and clean towels. Such facilities must be readily accessible to exposed employees and adequate for the number of employees exposed. The sanitation requirements for general industry and shipyards are similar to those for construction.

Hazard Communication (29 CFR 1926.59 for construction; 29 CFR 1910.1200 for general industry; 29 CFR 1915.1200 for shipyards) and Safety Training (29 CFR 1926.21 for construction)

The Hazard Communication standard requires that manufacturers and importers provide information on material safety data sheets (MSDSs) and labels about the hazards of portland cement. Employers must make these MSDSs and labels available to employees. The Hazard Communication and Safety Training standards also require employers to provide training to communicate the hazards of exposure to portland cement to their employees. This training must address:

- the hazards associated with exposure to portland cement, including hazards associated with the cement's Cr(VI) content;

- preventive measures, including proper use and care of PPE and the importance of proper hygiene practices; and

■ employee access to hygiene facilities, PPE, and information (including MSDSs).

Recordkeeping (29 CFR 1904)

Employers subject to OSHA recordkeeping requirements must inform employees of how to report work-related injuries and illnesses and record all new cases of work-related injury and illness (including cement burns and cases of dermatitis) that result in days away from work, restricted work or transfer to another job, medical treatment beyond first aid, or are otherwise determined to be a significant injury or illness by a physician or other licensed health care professional.

Permissible Exposure Limit (PEL) (29 CFR 1926.55 for construction; 29 CFR 1910.1000 for general industry; 29 CFR 1915.1000 for shipyards)

OSHA has established a permissible exposure limit to address the inhalation hazards of working with dry portland cement. Employers must limit airborne exposure to portland cement to 15 milligrams per cubic meter (mg/m^3) of air for total dust and 5 mg/m^3 for respirable dust. Because the Cr(VI) content in portland cement is so low, it is anticipated that by meeting the permissible exposure limit (PEL) of 15 mg/m^3 for portland cement, employers will also meet the Cr(VI) PEL and the action level of 5 and 2.5 micrograms per cubic meter ($\mu g/m^3$), respectively (see 1926.1126).

Preventing Cement-Related Skin Problems

The best way to prevent cement-related skin problems is to minimize skin contact with wet portland cement. Compliance with OSHA's requirements for provision of PPE, washing facilities, hazard communication and safety training, along with the good skin hygiene and work practices listed below, will protect against hazardous contact with wet cement.

Good Practices for Glove Selection and Use

- Provide the proper gloves for employees who may come into contact with wet portland cement. Consult the glove supplier or the cement manufacturer's MSDS for help in choosing the proper gloves. Butyl or nitrile gloves (rather than cotton or leather gloves) are frequently recommended for caustic materials such as portland cement.

- Use only well-fitting gloves. Loose-fitting gloves let cement in. Often the use of gloves and clothing makes exposure worse when cement gets inside or soaks through the garment. Use glove liners for added comfort.

- Wash hands before putting on gloves. Wash hands every time gloves are removed.

- Dry hands with a clean cloth or paper towel before putting on gloves.

- Protect arms and hands by wearing a long-sleeved shirt with the sleeves duct-taped to gloves to prevent wet cement from getting inside the gloves.

- Follow proper procedures for removing gloves, whether reusing or disposing them. See Table 1 at page 9 for proper procedures for removing gloves.

- Clean reusable gloves after use. Before removing gloves, clean the outside by rinsing or wiping off any wet cement. Follow the manufacturer's instructions for glove cleaning. Place clean and dry gloves in a plastic storage bag and store them in a cool, dry place away from tools.

- Throw out grossly contaminated or worn-out gloves.

- Keep the inside of gloves clean and dry.

- Do not use barrier creams or "invisible gloves." These products are not effective in protecting the skin from portland cement hazards.

Table 1. Steps for safe glove removal:

1. Wash off the outside of your gloves while you are still wearing them.

2. Loosen gloves on both hands, holding your arms down to prevent water from dripping onto the skin.

3. Holding your arms downward, pull the first glove down to remove only the glove fingers. The cuff should still be covering the palm of your hand.

4. Remove the second glove by grabbing it with the first glove.

5. Slip off the first glove.

6. Handle used gloves by the inside only.

Source: "Save Your Skin," CPWR, 2000b.

Good Practices for Use of Boots and Other Protective Clothing and Equipment

- Wear waterproof boots when necessary to prevent wet cement from coming into contact with skin. It is as important to protect legs, ankles, and feet from skin contact with wet cement as it is to protect hands.

- Boots need to be high enough to prevent wet cement from getting inside. Tuck pants inside and wrap duct tape around the top of the boots to prevent wet cement from entering.

- Select boots that are sturdy, strong enough to resist punctures and tears, and slip-resistant.

- Change protective boots if they become ineffective or contaminated on the inside with wet cement while in use.

- Change out of any work clothes that become contaminated with wet cement and keep contaminated work clothes separate from street clothes.

- When kneeling on wet cement use waterproof kneepads or dry kneeboards to prevent the knees from coming into contact with the cement.
- Wear proper eye protection when working with portland cement.

Good Practices for Skin Care

- Wash areas of the skin that come into contact with wet cement in clean, cool water. Use a pH-neutral or slightly acidic soap. Check with the soap supplier or manufacturer for information on the acidity and alkalinity of the soap.[2]
- Consider using a mildly acidic solution such as diluted vinegar or a buffering solution to neutralize caustic residues of cement on the skin.[3]
- Do not wash with abrasives or waterless hand cleaners, such as alcohol-based gels or citrus cleaners.
- Avoid wearing watches and rings at work since wet cement can collect under such items.
- Do not use lanolin, petroleum jelly, or other skin softening products. These substances can seal cement residue to the skin, increase the skin's ability to absorb contaminants, and irritate the skin. Skin softening products also should not be used to treat cement burns.

Making Portland Cement Products Less Hazardous

In recent decades there have been efforts to reduce the risk of developing cement-related skin problems by lowering the Cr(VI) content of portland cement. Cr(VI) is not intentionally added to portland cement and it does not serve any functional purpose. There are a variety of ways to minimize the amount of Cr(VI) in portland cement, including:

- Using slag, which is free of Cr(VI), in place of or blended with clinker, the primary source of Cr(VI) in portland cement. Slag is a by-product of the iron ore extraction process and has been used in concrete projects in the United States for over a century.

- Adding ferrous sulfate to portland cement may lower the Cr(VI) content of the cement. Use of ferrous sulfate has reportedly led to a decline in cases of allergic contact dermatitis in several countries (Goh et al., 1996; Avnstorp, 1989; Roto et al., 1996).[4]

Lowering the Cr(VI) content of portland cement can lessen, but not entirely eliminate, the risk of acquiring allergic contact dermatitis. It will not eliminate the other skin hazards posed by wet portland cement. Employers and employees need to take all necessary precautions to prevent skin contact with wet portland cement whether or not the cement contains measurable amounts of Cr(VI). Wearing proper gloves and other protective equipment, and following good skin care and work practices, provide the best protection against the skin hazards posed by wet portland cement.

In Agency for Toxic Substances and Disease Registry (ATSDR); "Toxicological profile for chromium"; *ATSDR Toxicological Profile,* 88/10, 2000; U.S. Public Health Service, Atlanta, GA.

Avnstorp, C.; "Prevalence of cement eczema in Denmark before and since addition of ferrous sulfate to Danish cement"; *Acta Demato-Venereologica,* 69(2), pp. 151-155, 1989; Stockholm.

Center to Protect Workers' Rights (CPWR) Consortium on Preventing Contact Dermatitis; *A Safety and Health Practitioner's Guide to Skin Protection,* 2000a; Researched, developed, and produced by FOF Communications; Available online at: http://www.cdc.gov/elcosh/docs/d0400/d000458/d000458.html. Also includes an employee safety pamphlet online at: http://www.cdc.gov/elcosh/docs/d0400/d000458/brochure.PDF, and http://www.cdc.gov/elcosh/docs/d0400/d000458/brochure2.PDF

CPWR; *Save Your Skin*; 2000b; Produced by FOF Communications; Available online at: http://www.cdc.gov/elcosh/docs/d0200/d000280/d000280.html

CPWR; *An Employer's Guide to Skin Protection,* 2000c; Researched, developed, and produced by FOF Communications; Available online at: http://www.cdc.gov/elcosh/docs/d0400/d000457/d000457.html

CPWR; *Save Your Skin: A 15-Minute Tool Box Session,* 2000d; Produced by FOF Communications; Available online at:

http://www.cdc.gov/elcosh/docs/d0300/d000303/d000303.html

"Comments of Building and Construction Trades Department, AFL-CIO, in Response to OSHA's Request for Comments on Exposure to Hexavalent Chromium"; Docket H-054a, Exhibit 31-6-1, pp. 7-8, November 19, 2002. (Re: OSHA's, "Occupational Exposure to Hexavalent Chromium (Cr(VI)), Request for Information"; *Federal Register,* 67 FR 54389-54394, August 22, 2002, (Exhibit 30).

CPWR; "Nonfatal Skin Diseases and Disorders in Construction"; *The Construction Chart Book, 3rd Edition,* Chapter 46, September 2002; CPWR is located in Silver Spring, MD.

Scientific Committee on Toxicity, Ecotoxicity and the Environment (CSTEE); *Opinion on Risks to Health from Chromium VI in Cement,* June 27, 2002; European Commission, Brussels.

De Raeve, H., Vandecasteele, C., Demedts, M., Nemery, B.; "Dermal and respiratory sensitization to chromate in a cement floorer"; *American Journal of Industrial Medicine,* 34(2), pp. 169-76, 1998.

Goh, C.L., Gan, S.L.; "Change in cement manufacturing process, a cause for decline in chromate allergy?"; *Contact Dermatitis,* 34(1), pp. 51-54, 1996; Munksgaard, Denmark.

Halbert, A.R., Gebauer, K.A., and Wall, L.M.; "Prognosis of occupational chromate dermatitis"; *Contact Dermatitis,* 27, pp. 214-219, 1992.

Helmuth, R.A., Miller, F.M., Greening, N.R., Hognestad, E., Kosmatka, S.H., Lang, D.; "Cement"; *Kirk-Othmer Encyclopedia of Chemical*

Technology., Volume 5, 4th edition, 1993; John Wiley & Sons, New York.

Irvine, C., Pugh, C.E., Hansen, E.J., and Rycroft, R.J.; "Cement dermatitis in underground workers during construction of the Channel Tunnel"; *Occupational Medicine,* 44(1), pp. 17-23, February 1994; London.

National Slag Association (NSA); *National Slag Association News, Publications, and Slag Industry Publications Archives;* West Lawn, PA; Available online at: http://www.nationalslag.org/

Occupational Safety and Health Administration; "Occupational Exposure to Hexavalent Chromium, Final Rule"; *Federal Register,* 71 FR 10100, February 28, 2006.

Rafnsson, V., Gunnarsdottir, H., Kiilunen, M.; "Risk of lung cancer among masons in Iceland"; *Occupational and Environmental Medicine,* 54(3), pp. 184-188, 1997.

Roto, P., Sainio, H., Reunala, T., Laippala, P.; "Addition of ferrous sulfate to cement and risk of chromium dermatitis among construction workers"; *Contact Dermatitis,* 34(1), pp. 43-50, 1996.

Sahai, D.; "Cement Hazards and Controls: Health Risks and Precautions in Using Portland Cement"; *Construction Safety Magazine,* 12(2), Summer 2001; Available at: http://www.cdc.gov/elcosh/docs/d0500/d000513/d000513.html

Shaw Environmental, Inc.; *Industry Profile, Exposure Profile, Technological Feasibility Evaluation, and Environmental Impact for Industries Affected by a Revised OSHA Standard for Hexavalent Chromium;* February 21, 2006; Shaw Environmental, Inc., 5050 Section Avenue, Cincinnati, Ohio, 45212.

Shepherd, L.; "Health in construction"; *The Safety & Health Practitioner,* 17(6), pp. 46-49, June 1999.

Slag Cement Association (SCA); "What is Slag Cement?" *Slag Cement;* Slag Cement Association, Sugar Land, Texas; Available online at: http://www.slagcement.org

Spoo, J. and P. Elsner; "Cement burns: a review 1960-2000"; *Contact Dermatitis,* 45(2), pp. 68-71, August 2001.

Stern, A.H., Bagdon, R.E., Hazen, R.E., Marzulli, F.N., 1993; "Risk assessment of the allergic dermatitis potential of environmental exposure to hexavalent chromium"; *Journal of Toxicology and Environmental Health,* 40(4), pp. 613-641, 1993.

Vickers, H.R., and Edwards, D.H.; "Cement burns"; *Contact Dermatitis,* 2, pp. 73-78, 1976.

Zachariae, C.O.C., Agner, T., and Menne, T.; "Chromium allergy in consecutive patients in a country where ferrous sulfate has been added to cement since 1981"; *Contact Dermatitis,* 35, pp. 83-85, 1996; Munksgaard, Denmark.

Technical Notes

[1] Hod carriers transport mortar, bricks, and concrete in a vee shaped trough (called a hod) to other employees.

[2] "An Employer's Guide to Skin Protection" (see CPWR, 2000c in the bibliography) contains a partial list of pH-neutral or moderately acidic liquid and bar soaps.

[3] "An Employer's Guide to Skin Protection" (see CPWR, 2000c in the bibliography) contains some information on neutralizing and buffering products.

[4] After Denmark required the addition of ferrous sulfate to reduce the Cr(VI) content of cement to less than 2 parts per million, studies showed a reduction in the prevalence of Cr(VI) allergy (Irvine et al., 1994). However, some U.S. cement manufacturers who have experimented with the use of ferrous sulfate have not been able to achieve significant Cr(VI) reduction. The reasons for this inability may be due to variations in the Cr(VI) content of cement and the amount of time that passes between cement manufacture and use. Time delays are an important consideration because ferrous sulfate may lose its effectiveness over time, depending on how cement is packaged and on humidity and temperature conditions during storage.

OSHA can provide extensive help through a variety of programs, including technical assistance about effective safety and health programs, state plans, workplace consultations, voluntary protection programs, strategic partnerships, training and education, and more. An overall commitment to workplace safety and health can add value to your business, to your workplace, and to your life.

Safety and Health Program Management Guidelines

Effective management of employee safety and health protection is a decisive factor in reducing the extent and severity of work-related injuries and illnesses and their related costs. In fact, an effective safety and health program forms the basis of good employee protection, can save time and money, increase productivity and reduce employee injuries, illnesses, and related workers' compensation costs.

To assist employers and employees in developing effective safety and health programs, OSHA published recommended Safety and Health Program Management Guidelines (54 *Federal Register* (16): 3904-3916, January 26, 1989). These voluntary guidelines can be applied to all places of employment covered by OSHA.

The guidelines identify four general elements critical to the development of a successful safety and health management system:

- Management leadership and employee involvement,
- Worksite analysis,
- Hazard prevention and control, and
- Safety and health training.

The guidelines recommend specific actions, under each of these general elements, to achieve an effective safety and health program. The *Federal Register* notice is available online at www.osha.gov.

State Programs

The Occupational Safety and Health Act of 1970 (OSH Act) encourages states to develop and operate their own job safety and health plans. OSHA approves and monitors these plans. Twenty-four states, Puerto Rico, and the Virgin Islands currently operate approved state plans: 22 cover both private and public (state and local government) employment; Connecticut, New Jersey, New York, and the Virgin Islands cover the public sector only. States and territories with their own OSHA-approved occupational safety and health plans must adopt standards identical to, or at least as effective as, the Federal OSHA standards.

Consultation Services

Consultation assistance is available on request to employers who want help in establishing and maintaining a safe and healthful workplace. Largely funded by OSHA, the service is provided at no cost to the employer. Primarily developed for smaller employers with more hazardous operations, the consultation service is delivered by state governments employing professional safety and health consultants. Comprehensive assistance includes an appraisal of all mechanical systems, work practices, and occupational safety and health hazards of the workplace and all aspects of the employer's present job safety and health program. In addition, the service offers assistance to employers in developing and implementing an effective safety and health program. No penalties are proposed or citations issued for hazards identified by the consultant. OSHA provides consultation assistance to the employer with the assurance that his or her name and firm and any information about the workplace will not be routinely reported to OSHA enforcement staff.

Under the consultation program, certain exemplary employers may request participation in OSHA's Safety and Health Achievement Recognition Program (SHARP). Eligibility for participation in SHARP includes receiving a comprehensive consultation visit, demonstrating exemplary achievements in workplace safety and health by abating all identified hazards, and developing an excellent safety and health program.

Employers accepted into SHARP may receive an exemption from programmed inspections (not complaint or accident investigation inspections) for a period of 1 year. For more information concerning consultation assistance, see OSHA's website at www.osha.gov.

Voluntary Protection Programs (VPP)

Voluntary Protection Programs and on-site consultation services, when coupled with an effective enforcement program, expand employee protection to help meet the goals of the OSH Act. The VPPs motivate others to achieve excellent safety and health results in the same outstanding way as they establish a cooperative relationship between employers, employees, and OSHA.

For additional information on VPP and how to apply, contact the OSHA regional offices listed at the end of this publication.

Strategic Partnership Program

OSHA's Strategic Partnership Program, the newest member of OSHA's cooperative programs, helps encourage, assist, and recognize the efforts of partners to eliminate serious workplace hazards and achieve a high level of employee safety and health. Whereas OSHA's Consultation Program and VPP entail one-on-one relationships between OSHA and individual worksites, most strategic partnerships seek to have a broader impact by building cooperative relationships with groups of employers and employees. These partnerships are voluntary, cooperative relationships between OSHA, employers, employee representatives, and others (e.g., trade unions, trade and professional associations, universities, and other government agencies).

For more information on this and other cooperative programs, contact your nearest OSHA office, or visit OSHA's website at www.osha.gov.

Alliance Program

Through the Alliance Program, OSHA works with groups committed to safety and health, including businesses, trade or professional organizations, unions and educational institutions, to leverage resources and expertise to develop compliance assistance tools and resources and share information with employers and employees to help prevent injuries, illnesses and fatalities in the workplace.

Alliance program agreements have been established with a wide variety of industries including meat, apparel, poultry, steel, plastics, maritime, printing, chemical, construction, paper and telecommunications. These agreements are addressing many safety and health hazards and at-risk audiences, including silica, fall protection, amputations, immigrant workers, youth and small businesses. By meeting the goals of the Alliance Program agreements (training and education, outreach and communication, and promoting the national dialogue on workplace safety and health), OSHA and the Alliance Program participants are developing and disseminating compliance assistance information and resources for employers and employees such as electronic assistance tools, fact sheets, toolbox talks, and training programs.

OSHA Training and Education

OSHA area offices offer a variety of information services, such as compliance assistance, technical advice, publications, audiovisual aids, and speakers for special engagements. OSHA's Training Institute in Arlington Heights, IL, provides basic and advanced courses in safety and health for Federal and state compliance officers, state consultants, Federal agency personnel, and private sector employers, employees, and their representatives.

The OSHA Training Institute also has established OSHA Training Institute Education Centers to address the increased demand for its courses from the private sector and from other federal agencies. These centers include colleges, universities, and nonprofit training organizations that have been selected after a competition for participation in the program.

OSHA also provides funds to nonprofit organizations, through grants, to conduct workplace training and education in subjects where OSHA believes there is a lack of workplace training. Grants are awarded annually. Grant recipients are expected to contribute 20 percent of the total grant cost.

For more information on training and education, contact the OSHA Training Institute, Directorate of Training and Education, 2020 South Arlington Heights Road, Arlington Heights, IL, 60005, (847) 297-4810, or see Training on OSHA's website at www.osha.gov. For further information on any OSHA program, contact your nearest OSHA regional office listed at the end of this publication.

Information Available Electronically

OSHA has a variety of materials and tools available on its website at www.osha.gov. These include electronic compliance assistance tools, such as *Safety and Health Topics Pages, eTools, Expert Advisors;* regulations, directives, publications and videos; and other information for employers and employees. OSHA's software programs and compliance assistance tools walk you through challenging safety and health issues and common problems to find the best solutions for your workplace.

A wide variety of OSHA materials, including standards, interpretations, directives, and more can be purchased on CD-ROM from the U.S. Government Printing Office, Superintendent of Documents, toll-free phone (866) 512-1800.

OSHA Publications

OSHA has an extensive publications program. For a listing of free items, visit OSHA's website at www.osha.gov or contact the OSHA Publications Office, U.S. Department of Labor, 200 Constitution Avenue, NW, N-3101, Washington, DC 20210; telephone (202) 693-1888 or fax to (202) 693-2498.

Contacting OSHA

To report an emergency, file a complaint, or seek OSHA advice, assistance, or products, call (800) 321-OSHA or contact your nearest OSHA Regional office listed at the end of this publication. The teletypewriter (TTY) number is (877) 889-5627.

Written correspondence can be mailed to the nearest OSHA Regional or Area Office listed at the end of this publication or to OSHA's national office at: U.S. Department of Labor, Occupational Safety and Health Administration, 200 Constitution Avenue, N.W., Washington, DC 20210.

By visiting OSHA's website at www.osha.gov, you can also:

- File a complaint online,
- Submit general inquiries about workplace safety and health electronically, and
- Find more information about OSHA and occupational safety and health.

Region I
(CT,* ME, MA, NH, RI, VT*)
JFK Federal Building, Room E340
Boston, MA 02203
(617) 565-9860

Region II
(NJ,* NY,* PR,* VI*)
201 Varick Street, Room 670
New York, NY 10014
(212) 337-2378

Region III
(DE, DC, MD,* PA, VA,* WV)
The Curtis Center
170 S. Independence Mall West
Suite 740 West
Philadelphia, PA 19106-3309
(215) 861-4900

Region IV
(AL, FL, GA, KY,* MS, NC,* SC,* TN*)
61 Forsyth Street, SW, Room 6T50
Atlanta, GA 30303
(404) 562-2300

Region V
(IL, IN,* MI,* MN,* OH, WI)
230 South Dearborn Street
Room 3244
Chicago, IL 60604
(312) 353-2220

Region VI
(AR, LA, NM,* OK, TX)
525 Griffin Street, Room 602
Dallas, TX 75202
(972) 850-4145

Region VII
(IA,* KS, MO, NE)
Two Pershing Square
2300 Main Street, Suite 1010
Kansas City, MO 64108-2416
(816) 283-8745

Region VIII
(CO, MT, NO, SO, UT,* WY*)
1999 Broadway, Suite 1690
PO Box 46550
Denver, CO 80202-5716
(720) 264-6550

Region IX
(AZ,* CA,* HI,* NV,* and American Samoa,
Guam and the Northern Mariana Islands)
90 7th Street, Suite 18-100
San Francisco, CA 94103
(415) 625-2547

Region X
(AK,* ID, OR,* WA*)
1111 Third Avenue, Suite 715
Seattle, WA 98101-3212
(206) 553-5930

* These states and territories operate their own
OSHA-approved job safety and health programs and
cover state and local government employees as well as
private sector employees. The Connecticut, New Jersey,
New York and Virgin Islands plans cover public employees only. States with approved programs must have
standards that are identical to, or at least as effective as,
the Federal standards.

Note: To get contact information for OSHA Area
Offices, OSHA-approved State Plans and OSHA
Consultation Projects, please visit us online at
www.osha.gov or call us at 1-800-321-0SHA.